EXPLORING *this* TERRAIN

Poems

Margaret B. Ingraham

PARACLETE PRESS
BREWSTER, MASSACHUSETTS

2020 First Printing

Exploring this Terrain: Poems

Copyright © 2020 by Margaret Ingraham

ISBN 978-1-64060-376-9

Library of Congress Cataloging-in-Publication Data
Names: Ingraham, Margaret B., author.
Title: Exploring this terrain: poems / Margaret Ingraham.
Description: Brewster : Paraclete Press, 2020. | Summary: "These poems
  cross the beautiful landscape of wonder, the uneven country of love, the
  difficult ground of faith"— Provided by publisher.
Identifiers: LCCN 2019048927 (print) | LCCN 2019048928 (ebook) | ISBN
  9781640603769 (trade paperback) | ISBN 9781640603776 (mobi) | ISBN
  9781640603783 (epub) | ISBN 9781640603790 (pdf)
Subjects: LCGFT: Poetry.
Classification: LCC PS3609.N4675 E97 2020 (print) | LCC PS3609.N4675
  (ebook) | DDC 811/.6—dc23
LC record available at https://lccn.loc.gov/2019048927
LC ebook record available at https://lccn.loc.gov/2019048928

10 9 8 7 6 5 4 3 2 1

Published by Paraclete Press
Brewster, Massachusetts
www.paracletepress.com

Printed in the United States of America

In memory of Chip and of Phyllis
with gratitude
and
for Madeleine Grace

CONTENTS

"For you shall go out in joy
and be led forth in peace;
the mountains and the hills before you
shall break forth into singing,
and all the trees of the field shall clap their hands."

Isaiah 55:12

I

IN MOUNTAINS' SHADE

*"In his hands are the depths of the earth;
the heights of the mountains are his also."*

Psalm 95:4

Proverbs

"[Silence] is the fence around wisdom."
—Ancient Hebrew Proverb

"Doth not wisdom cry,
and understanding put forth her voice?
She standeth in the top of high places,
By the way in the places of the paths."
—Proverbs 8:1–2

Yesterday was clear
and warmer than we would expect
this time of year
on the lip of Blue Ridge.
Bull bellowed through the afternoon
and the Little Dipper
tipped a glimmer from beneath
the gauze of stratus curtain
blowing in.

By morning clouds had settled
and an odd mockingbird came quietly
to sip remnants of rain
from the cement planter
out beside the corncrib,
and all four of them—
cloud, bird, stained water, concrete box—
carried the same inference
of gray.

Although I waited all day
for the familiarity of winter
shadows dropping long, falling dark,
before they would finally recede,
nothing moved across the field
except the breeze,
nothing met me on the path
except westerly wind turning in
at dusk.

I know that night will show itself
this way along the high ridge
of Mt. San Angelo:
pillar of cloud will dissolve
into the gray solitude of cattle
sighing and that mysterious wisdom
we came here to know
will slip invisibly inside
silence's fence.

Transfiguration

Spring moves up the ridge at the rate
of 100 feet per day in the Shenandoah.

Thus it is that, without asking,
spring moves up the ridge
another day's full measure,
so cowslip carpets a high meadow
that yesterday lay a plain new green.
Redbuds that hailed the end of frosts
now pale beside the flowering quince
and blaze of samara seeds like blood
red wings adorn the supplicant limbs
of winter-weary sugar maple
and, without asking, pull my gaze
far from valley seam to move me
with this season's rite procession
up distant hills where purple hurt
like Shenandoah's haze recedes
into this broken night and through
ragged strips of gauzy clouds
the paschal wafer moon
washes the whole prospect
in ambient glow of its topaz light.

Evensong

This far north
it is still South Holston waters
clucking softly on the rocks
like a small coop of contented hens
at roosting time.

Deep in the circles of evening
all the leg-singing crickets
gather on the shore
to play new melodies
with their knees.

In these mountains
they say
you must always come alone
to dance a summer polka
to the Blue Ridge crickets' song.

The Thrush of Morning

In this fourth month's first day's
new light, I walk the familiar path
that is still damp with early mists,
which seem forever reticent
to dissipate and let the morning in.
Just as they, I hesitate along the slope
at the place the gravel footpath forks
and listen a moment for the hidden thrush,
although I know it's well ahead
of time for its migratory visit here;
in that pause I think of lonesome Keats—
who named another season for these fogs—
and of his nightingale, whose songs
he heard, though bird he could not see.
Disappointed that this dawn brings
no melody or hint of morning song to me,
I turn beneath my longing to discover
in the lifting haze the season's recompense
left last night under a starless cover—
delicate green stoles of finely knotted buds
draped over grand Chinese elms' low boughs
and young curly willows' sloping shoulders,
new leaves waving hosannas in a secret breeze,
ushering in the promise of days more lush
than these, fuller hedges to hide the timid vireo
and pledge of dulcet notes more tuneful
than ever the ancient dancing flutists piped.
I keep this silence to myself, a quiet
like the one Keats understood could make
sheer mornings such as this seem bittersweet.

Postcard from the Blue Ridge

Do you recall which of these was O'Keeffe's mountain? I have
been looking out on them all week and am still not sure, perhaps
because I am facing from the south. But I do understand now
why she kept coming back to paint here, where from hour to
hour they are never the same mountains—although they
constantly abide. And there's no contradiction in it. Ridge after
ridge grows paler in the farther light so the eye is finally driven
to the fine abstraction, appearing almost as remembrance (as
fine as Keats' excess, and maybe that is the place where painter
and poet meet) that the vista holds. After A.S. or anyone and
everyone else, for that matter, it must have been what she was
painting for: to find, as we have, what holds.

Beholding Nehemiah

Morning's a pale entrance
and so we traipse
the trail in diffuse mist
outside the slack wire fence
where the cows stand.
She is a large, white milker;
he, smaller than the heifers.
We call him Nehemiah.
Her, we give no name.
All the same she moves
to him and he falls still
under the broad spell
of mothering tongue,
nuzzling his nape, caressing
his crown, tender behind his ear,
then soft to forehead, neck again,
incessant on his cheek.
She is encompassing. He accepts
all he has ever known. Only we
seek meaning in the mysterious
moment we behold mother
and son, beautiful and bonding,
bound to breaking.

Picture Postcard from VA — Winter Landscape

Thought you'd want to know that Nehemiah's gone—
moved, I have to trust, to another farm. The cows and other
calves are pastured now across the road, and all of them are
blonde (but more the color of buttermilk than the light of
your hair). As you've always said, nuances disappear in
monochrome, so it is still hard for me to tell these little
ones apart. All in all, this early winter has not been as
welcoming as last, until today's blowing snow. Under its
brush even the restless bull is stroked into a muslin silence,
perplexed at how quickly the drifts cover the plain umber
of the farm's underpainting and alter his terrain. Or so it
seems. I am not sure whether I favor the familiar landscape
or this one, or in which of the two I can more easily lose
myself . . . as I came here to do. That, and write, of course—
for which I am primed. But once again I am falling behind in
my promises and wondering, as always, just what you
would make of it all.

Ordinary Time

Just as I lamented the cloud cover,
the forecast for another rainy day,
she chided me, said yesterday
had been so glorious, not for lack
of rain, though there'd been none,
but because last week there'd come
torrents to green the lawn
and nudge the buds along.

Just as I spoke, the sun emerged
again, began, almost proverbially,
another minuet with vernal fog,
its opening of the grand dance hall
to the crowds of chirping passerines.
And the groundhog I had not seen
this month came scuttling happily
along the perimeter of the tottering barn.

In this light I question how to hold
blessings such as these in trembling
hands, can barely understand as today
ends in a pink-robed gloaming,
where ordinary time concludes
and season of bright gratitude begins.
I have seen creation show itself
pristine, and I know that it is good.

Overlooking Shenandoah

*"Please don't get close to fawns lying curled
and still. . . . They can be easily separated
from their mothers."*
—Shenandoah Overlook, Summer 2002

Even out beyond this fawning season
They still must lean upon their own
Keen sense of reckoning
To appraise each unforeseen approach —
Ours or cunning snake's
Or sudden thunderhead's
Or vagrant lightning bolt's.

For such are the ways
Of these blue slopes:
And how the redtails hover
Inside the wind-banked troughs;
And how softly the does move
To rouse callow ones to cover;
How moss cleaves to the west
Face of the trunks like men
Cling closely to their lore.

There are no clear divisions here
Where elevations gradually descend
And range extends beyond sheer overlook;
No easy ways to separate mere mists
From Shenandoah's dawn
Or drowsy warble from the vireo
Or doe from spotted fawn.

At the Memorial

After the embracing of the widow and children,
the telling of stories, the reading of the poem,
the dedication of the bench and tree, there in
the blued shadow of the high ridge's own garden
we sat down together to eat, though some of us
strangers, as friends, feasting once more on
the recollection of full-bellied joy he always served
up silently in mounds of fried chicken and macaroni
and cheese. As if a sequitur his older sister pointed
to the early thin shoots of the golden forsythia that
rattled against the glass vase's lip in the subtle breeze
and said, "When these bloom it's time to start cutting
back the roses again." And I and the others, who knew
nothing of that, nodded to the certain gardener's
plain-spoken confidence of sequencing: plant, nurture,
behold the glory in the bloom, prune, and then expect
a fuller blossoming again.

II

ALL THE WATER TOUCHES

*"The sea is his, for he made it,
and his hands formed the dry land."*

Psalm 95:5

Observances
for Phyllis

i.
At dawn there are the shorebirds
after silent matins—
a colony of common gulls,
two whimbrels and a plover—
genuflecting above the shining sand
while they seek their portions.

ii.
The breeze that moved so gently
over deep with morning's haste
gusts up again to chase the birds
and raise the drowsy heads of sea oats
bending to the dunes and rouse
them into rhythmic davening.

iii.
At height of sun and breaking tide
the boat-tailed grackle all alone
has found assurance bold enough
to trawl the rippled shallows of the strand
and harrow their more plenteous supply
than any need he seeks to satisfy.

iv.
The spirited wind at last subsides
to allow the angling tide to roll
the foamy edges of the ocean back
then suddenly picks up again
to lift a string of pelicans and ferry them
along the secret way of glimmering fish.

v.

All the while the understated moon
waits for hibiscus cast
of journeying sun to nestle
behind the shadow of scrub pines
before it puts its own reflection down
on the stiller surface of the sound.

These are the fixed hours on the outer banks
a single page within the endless book of days
creation follows to render praise
and recognize the power that abides.
And this is mystery akin to grace
how water and wind and bird together
all converge in this one place
where with this liturgy of light
I come to see
what holds them all keeps me.

Moving from Deep

the ocean gust raises the flag
of my small dog's tail
just as it plumes
the heads of sea oats
clinging to dunes,
billows them both as if
there were no difference
between what is new and impetuous
and what is familiar and rooted
for it is neither,
this wind.

Tidewater

Here is Northern Neck's
typology at spring's approach —
spindly forsythia and wild mustard
are first to encroach against the raw
umbers and dull ochres of mud and marsh.
Tributaries flow to estuaries running
to rivers feeding the bay that openly
gives herself up to the larger body,
all fingers of water that move subtly
toward the trigger points, loosen
every strain an outsider brings,
yet have somehow lost all touch
to soothe commonwealth's lowland ennui
and cannot stop the anxious oysterman
from monotonously declaring that surely
by now, when winter has had its way
and the goats have stripped the forage,
it is futile to make the same climb again
up the crooked rungs of makeshift ladders
nailed to live oak and yellow pine
and into the deer stands just to wait
through one more vacant morning.
"Better ways to pass the time, "
I heard one of them say.
"No reason not to let the beagles in
with the fenced foxes" to test them
for right instincts, hope to find
the kind of grit they count on
from the native hounds—
how they lock on the scent,
keep their heads down,

hold their noses to the ground,
stay dead set on the trail
despite every distraction,
just like that fine farmer's pack
did five Aprils ago now
when it missed the vixen that crossed
from the wood and ran three full circles
through the rutted field,
spiraling toward the center
where she stood safe in the open,
because the whole lot of them
were hell-bent on making
every perfect inbred turn.

Resemblance

These are the perspectives from the dunes:

first, after dawn's terns have flown
black cormorant owns the whole horizon,
plunges headlong into the roiling surf,
and neatly plucks a slender fish
that for an instant on the surface
flails, a sterling flash, in the blaze
of noon sun's harsh broad glare;

and there, in the same place by night,
the moon makes light of midday scene
and over the dark serene prospect
casts down near celestial beams,
trailing myriad minute specks
that lay soft silver crescents
across reflective breaker caps;

now here, atop the great sand hill,
I am drawn to wondering
how just a single fleck of glitter
that moon casts on pitching waves
can so perfectly resemble
the last desperate twitch and jitter
of one silent dying fish.

From the dunes at distant ends
of these spectral lights
I have seen them mirror dancing,
vying for attention once again,
those ancient estranged twins:
the fleet brazen one named terror
and the stunning one called awe.

Echo Song

We sit in the stillest place
Where mountains wall horizon
On three sides
Majestic lodge pole pines
Look small against the sill
Tree and rock together
Throw our voices back
Across the watery flat.

A solitary loon
Starts from the shallows
Skims above the lake
Hearing only the echo song
His wings make
To gauge the depth
He settles on before
He takes a needle dive
To thread the undercurrents
Then surfaces again
Beside the reeds
That bend astonished
In the furtive wind.

Twilight pours honey glaze
Across this place
And night moves on
Still we sit
We need not ask the loon
To wait until the stars
And moon are set
To hide again
We cannot ask
For more than this.

Empty Chamber

Abandoned by the conch
the shell becomes memory
holding the roll of sea
in the scroll of its cell
sifting monotonous rhythms
from waters around its bed.
The moon drags the depths
and reveals a storied surface:
layers of barnacles,
edges broken in the fall
against the reef.

Its chronicle is myth
spilling a chambered history
like evening's, like a man's,
an anthem that repeats
the easy sounding
of horizon breaking against sky
waves running to strands,
an echo that mysteriously forgets
wild surf's awful pounding
that tossed it aimlessly
on this deserted shoal.

Ode for a Crossing Fox

Four days I passed along that spit of land
between the ocean dunes and barriered sound
and saw him lying there. I thought him bound
inland as tides, and yet he faced instead

surely windward toward the coastal side.
Four days I passed. The first, he seemed at rest,
his coat still quick against the marshy grain.
The second day his flesh held tight as dream,

as firm as sleep, his eyes remained yet deep.
The third it was the grackle came, walked wide
about but did not light. Then that night brought
a rain that spanned the brim of the fourth day

and left him changed, his skin as unrestrained
as loose cadences of the wind that played
from sea again across the slender bed
the tender hands of grass had shaped for him.

Four days I passed alone and saw at last
from my remove just how perfect stillness
would prove the ease of time in taking him,
out of sleek posture and his sure intent

would move him out of fractured circumstance
above the place where danger always danced,
would guide us both beyond what finally seemed
the strange ungainliness of his decease,

leading leeward over the fenny plain
of nesting plover, into thick forest's
cover and west into the hinterland,
boundless beyond the estuarine sound.

Preservation

for three named Charles

My brother's son
barely knew our father
and never heard him say
when he was young
and the sky was clear
enough so that the moon
brightened the beach,
it was all he needed
to follow her deep tracks
and see where she nested
her eggs in the dry sand.
And he would stand
looking toward the tide
and think about the day
some would know the way
and scurry toward water
to hide in Sargasso weed
where they would feed
for decades until they grew
large and strong as the ones
that let him climb upon
their heavy carapaces to ride
along at labored pace
what seemed like miles
across the barren sands.

My only brother's only son
patrols the wide shore
of a different land
searching for a single clutch
of hope from which to take
in hand and point
toward the sea enough
of the tiny leatherbacks
to keep safe for another
century the preserve
of a small posterity—
his grandfather's near dream
of him, of them, side-by-side
astride the great sea turtles
gliding toward moonlit waves
diving like the dolphin-riding
boys of lost Atlantis
into the briny myths
of an enduring deep.

III

THIS SMALL PLOT

*"Remember the former things
of old."*

Isaiah 46:9

Great Blue in the Cemetery

What brought you to this land-locked place
of stones carved out rectangular
and set down hard against a ground
laced with thin coverlet of pine,
needles shining fine as amber
beneath a trace of late December frost?
What kept you here to watch
my annual return to this small lot
from which I'm hewn and still
the only place for me to move
alone through generations left to right—
husband, wife, father, mother—
toward the pause by which my single plight
will break not heart so much as perfect alternation?

Surely none of that escaped
the sliver pierce of your gold heron eye
and yet you were not moved at all
by that or bite of season or bitter wind
the cloudless azure southern sky belied.
From where you gravely stood on poker leg
you must have heard me speak their names,
and must have watched me clear the plot,
and take in hand a year's full residue
of twigs and cones and fallen bark,
and sweep them off without my glove,
and press my palm against ancestral stones
to push away the cold that time insists
to leave and rocks agree to hold.

There you were solitary witness
to the solemn rite that I had thought
I was observing fully out of sight
of any other being, and yet seeing that
is what made you wait my notice
before you opened yourself up to flight,
unfolded the great span of your blue wings
that left shuddering in their wake
all bound and weighted things —
a marble angel tilted on headstone's crown
and me, bent down whispering and chilled
and yearning to secure everything
our visitations bring and all we take
from such a strange winter meeting place.

Crossing

Saturday I went out early, hoping to save
my ailing garden from the clutch of drought,
and focused as I was on the parched leaves
and the browning grasses, I still heard
the whirring of the hummingbird
as he made his easy passes between
the limbs of maple and crab apple,
and caught a quick iridescent flash
before he darted behind the ash, around
the pine and climbed completely out of sight.

Just before fall of dusk, it must have been,
I went out again to look for summer clouds
or any sign at all of rain and at about
the height I'd witnessed the hummer's fading
I saw that one great blue heron moving
without sound, deliberate and majestic,
like some crown royalty, avian queen or king
of the close realm of wetlands and of open air,
crossing from here to there mysteriously.

So it was at day's end, as at its beginning,
that they appeared so gracefully above
my small place of dust and dying shrub—
a huge heron and a minute ruby throat—
the greater and the lesser of the birds,
neither one expected, and neither one
of them known either for sustenance
or for song, and yet that day they were
for me both sweet manna on the wing
and melody beyond any longing.

Clearing

On these mornings
still beneath hoarfrost
I observe where
the deer have followed
the path we made
how my small hound
keen on a scent
steps precisely along
the cobbled line
of river stones
how they move
oblivious to us
as minor prophets
awaiting an opening
willing to risk
any turn in yearn
of finding
wind's constant way
toward the clearing.

Thanksgiving Morning

Right where the field slopes up
near the plain beginning of the narrow wood
I stood alone and caught
the ember edge of orange dawn
smoldering the charred heart
out of the hard log of night.
As I watched sheer morning slowly seep
toward the broad feet of lichened trunks,
a spirited rustling disturbed the underbrush,
then stopped the moment I looked up.
There between the thin bare arms
of the young trees she gradually appeared
in light so flat and low at first she seemed a shadow
except her eyes betrayed her solid presence.
Then I was rapt in her pure vigilance
intent on probing the full extent of danger
I might pose to her or the brash fawn
I could not see but sensed her holding close.
So we both stood transfixed
until I let the weight of obligation pull me back
to all the customary duties of that day.
I know she watched me go and
walk the full length of the field.
I know she never turned to seek refuge.
I'm telling you she did not stir nor stray
from the patient way she knew:
perfect deliverance had always come for her
in waiting still right where she stood.

Remembering Papa

My bedroom was on the back side
of the house so I could see him exit
the screen porch before the others heard
the loose-hinged door slam against the jamb
and know he'd headed to the yard
with his favorite rod in hand to cast
the heavy lures toward the stand
of ivy-circled pines that through
every season held their color fast.

No one ever dared approach him there
fearing they might invade the pact
of solitude he had made with the brief light
of those late autumn afternoons.
But I would race out of my back door
and wait behind him on the side
opposite his angling arm
until he'd reeled the line back in
and turned then to motion me to him.

His words were always as sure
as the grip he kept upon the rod:
Look at the way the shaft narrows
at the end and how much room
each guide gives the thin line to move.
An angler knows just how to space his leads
and that without the proper weights
on the line it is purposeless to try to fish.
He knows just where to place his toss
to fool the bass and draw them to the shallows.
He teaches himself to read light and shadows.

Now I drift our secret coves alone,
now mine, in silence as he taught
that all good fishermen must do.
By memory I see his silver skiff
as it drifts toward dim horizon line.
His dip net shimmers when he lays it down.
Then he leans across the oarlock to ease
the gasping smallmouth back into cool water,
looks up and signals to me with his hands.

Morning Business

> *"I know all the birds of the hills,*
> *and all that moves in the field is mine."*
> —Psalm 50:11

The ritual of my daily walk
across this ordinary yard
was morning opening to light
melodies of the small birds,
of finch and wren and chickadee
whose sweet soft calls were overtures
before the raucous solo of the crow
at whose cawing I would stop
and turn toward the briery hedge
where from the shadowed edge
the hesitant rabbit would angle
slowly down the gentle slope of hill
bound peculiarly to its twitching rhythm
and disappear into blackberry thicket.

But today that rabbit burst
from the canopy of familiar shade
and headed straight toward the clearing
as though it had some business there.
Then in its dark majesty
the waiting Cooper's hawk
swooped with perfect aim
from far atop the locust grove
past a young pair of hickories
and down into the meadow grass.

So quietly did the small hare fall
even the crass swaggering crow
silenced its monotonous squawk.
As quiet fed the hungering hawk
serenity lay like a strange pall
across the coarse terrain of all
the crow and I had watched.

Unraveling the Riddle of our Sphinx
for Meg

Remember in the haze of summer evening,
when the moon was weakly falling back
behind the humid weight of August air,
as we sat talking we sensed some strange
other presence there and heard the whirring
of the wings before we ever saw the thing
dart resolutely toward the purple petunias
cascading over the edge of a planter box?

"Hummingbird," I said. "Ruby-throated
but female, I am sure, it is so pale;
even in this dusky light the gorget
would flash red, if it were male."
Hers was a hypnotic flight that held
us spellbound as she hovered
above each bloom, stealing nectar
from the depths of blossom's core
until, as mysteriously as she'd come,
she turned and flitted at a distance past
nimbus of light around the glass hurricane,
not drawn in by candle's rippling flame
but satisfied enough to travel on.
Then we saw she was not bird at all
but some dull imposter who had dared
beguile us with her artful flight
not for our pleasure but for herself
in surrender to the thing she was.

Months or years later I chanced to find
a warning in the definitive field guide,
a note that even expert birders often
wrongly identify those nocturnal visitors:
"Large sphinx moths (*sphingidae*)
might be mistaken for hummers,
but seldom visit flowers before dusk."

We were clearly taught that much
but missed, I think, the writer's afterthought:
"The routine acts of nature might be
mistaken for a kind of splendor,
but rarely are they recognized as such."

The more costly mistake, it seems
to me, is losing what we hoped to see
by allowing a lantern's consuming light
to transform wonder we beheld that night
into nothing more than common sight.

After the Diagnosis

there were no more arguments
and the house next door
seemed far too quiet
to be the place
I had always known
except that evening when
for a few hours respite
my father and his sisters
and their mother left me
alone there to sit with him
and agony no doctor could tame
wrenched his gut and he let go
a sound I could neither name
nor tell anyone else about
not then not now not anymore
than I can explain how
to parse the strange syntax
of love and pain
of light and dark.

To Paint the Purple Finch

When the purple finch clamped himself to the limb
of my butterfly bush, one day last May I think, and there
against the flowering branch looked more a magenta hue
than his name construed—and both were so beautiful
and nimble, he in his instinctive grasp and it in its submissive
sway beneath the wind—I thought I should sketch out
the elements of the scene, longing then not just to memorize
that moment but, as I still do now, to paint that purple finch.
At once I realized the impossibility and began to reason
out my limitations, my utter lack of skill with parsing
and paring perspective and of artfully articulating the space
beyond foreground. Perceiving right horizon—the manner
and place in which it is marked and measured; and how we,
each of us, see it from our fixed positions; and foremost
how deftly painters take that complex concept in hand
and reduce it to one prime horizontal line, by reference
to which the painting's universe is then defined—
was too perplexing. I could not settle absolutely on just one.
Nor could the finch, which took wing on a late buoying current
of the subsiding wind and caught my eye again and held it
close until his tiny crescent torso was lost in what seemed
to me the reaches of oblivion but rather were to him
the thousand places at least that he could see
earth and sky meet.

IV

THE COMPANY OF WOMEN

"Strength and dignity are her clothing,
and she laughs at the time to come."

Proverbs 31:25

IV

Certainty

Certain things my mother knew
and she would not forget them:
like the scent magnolias take
when the sun has pressed
its full weight down inside
the cup of blossom long enough
to spring the hinges
of every creamy petal
and turn each one to chamois cloth,
beige and soft;
or the sunset glow
of tufted titmouse breast;
or mystery of kestrel's flight
soaring to crescendo height when
still wings dangle dangerously
on the precipice of fickle breeze.

Mother lived to open up the world to us
in things that always closed
or hid or ebbed away:
like frothy lace the small waves
tool along the sand at turn of tide;
or caddis fly's empty case
clinging to the smooth flat belly
of a stone in running shallows;
or tender young mimosa leaves curling
to put themselves to sleep
when we'd brush our tiny palms
across the smallest fronds.

These were the things, my mother said,
that nature always ordered
and on which we could depend.

Yesterday I wandered off
the well-marked trail
lured by the hope of hearing
low lamentations of the mourning dove
or distinct call of black-capped chickadee,
tones that float effortlessly
from small birds' quivering throats.
Instead the clearest sound I heard
was one I'd thought endangered long ago:
arduous and heavy-headed hammering
only a pileated woodpecker makes
when it has found the restive beetle
burrowing down inside a dying trunk.

This, of course, was part of what she knew:
some things open,
others close,
and certain things abide.

Of Moment

Does it matter where the birds go? Does it even matter
What species they are?
They leave here, that's the point,
First their bodies, then their sad cries.
—Louise Glück, "Parable of Flight"

Knowing your fondness for her and your walks together
through the woods, I admit I was surprised to learn
that you did not share her fascination with the birds.
There is certainly no point in trying to argue you
into that now. But I will make the case that it does matter
what species the birds are. Finches are not falcons
and no wren, or even mockingbird for that matter,
can mimic the heron's shriek. Nor is it their leaving
that is of consequence; their departures are so little different
from our own, except that ours are more easily described
as pointless or necessary, inevitable or untimely. Rather
the import is in their returning: how buntings, for example,
brood after long forgotten brood, maintain forever
their migratory fidelity, often guided by Polaris, other times
by path integration so that their navigation is at once celestial
and dead reckoning, and so that those differing methods
coalesce into a single predictable mystery that defies us,
even as it kindles our anticipation and defines our desire
to reclaim the first sighting, as when she grasped
your tiny wrist with one hand and pointed to the poplar
branch with the other. Whether I tell it like this or
fashioned into some private parable, one thing is certain:
the moment is in their coming once more by memory—
theirs and ours.

Even

Even in her Alzheimer's
my mother still loved the pansies
talked incessantly about them
made sure that I understood
how they survived every winter
in the garden of my childhood home
and later asked me again and again
again and again just to make sure
I could see how the blossoms
had bright faces ("oh, mercy,
how smiles do become both blooms
and girls," she was ever saying)
small faces that never changed
not even through all the afternoons
she spent softly talking to them
not even when she sat in silence
staring toward the bed emptied
by a deep hard freeze and turning
expressionless from then on
her countenance never changing
my mother loved the faces of pansies
because they had the quiet grace
to console to conceal every grief
is what I think my mother meant
to say to me when she turned away
hoping one last time to find
their glorious faces even then.

Vanished Light

The wooden point of her brush
Etches hieroglyphics
Into the damp paint
Of her canvas:
Layers planed in new colors
Each time she imagines earth
Opening like a quartered orange
To bare its sections,
The strata she lays flat
With facile strokes.

Perspective shifts like the hills
When the clouds move
Each time she squeezes new oil
From old tubes
To rework definitions,
Marks she makes
In the studied space
Between umbers
Where shadows always fall back
After vanished light.

Her eye, the brush, her hand
Are three points of the prism
Translating white to spectrum
And ordering all the lines
To reshape the entire scheme
Of time and tint and distance.

The Nellie Mae Fragments

i

PERENNIAL

Her tinder box house
the tint of rain
sinks early behind
blue hydrangea shadow.

Inside she sleeps for sorrow,
dreams the secret of color
that she alone knows:
her husband driving
iron three pennies
deep into black soil
beside the root
to hold the first placed hue.

The bed is empty
but currant bushes
need little tending:
hydrangeas reach to eaves,
grow deeper with the rust
he set in the dusty plot
that is her lot.

ii
THAW

Her husband left too soon
only footprints and a pot-bellied stove
heating the inner room
when she finds kindling.

Night spins from her head like a broken top
rattling warped floorboards.
She stirs, touches the cool black neck
for warmth opens the door
squints for bright edges of wood.

Dawn's starling call lures her to the street.
But trumpet vines entwine the gate
and she must wait the spring
to snap the twigs, free the swing to go.

Two Women

When she gave herself to Bach
she became two women:
impassioned one,
swaying her small frame
into the swell
of the concerto's movement
following sharp allegro taps
that her flirtatious fingers
lay against bright ivory;
the other, deliberate as she was,
patiently measuring out adagio strokes
that left her slender wrists
curving in the air
and drifting back.

Remembering where first
his hands had moved,
she let herself become
firm and fragile music
and played out,
note by note,
both what she was
and what she could be
only for him.

Dark Intersection
for Holly (1957–1978)

You were watching the moon
when you left the road
to take the ravine
where the soft red Georgia mud
whispered to you
as Chickasaw songs
the ancient names
of these hills, that place,
and called your crimson shadow
to mark a richer spot
in the dim half-light
where it fell
like you casually.

Winter comes always
winding its own path
bringing to evergreen shrubs
slick bright berries
that stir your name.
We call into the wind
follow the veil of breath
the lengthening days
as far as we can
but May always edges us
off the trail, stops us
at the place we find
the moon is holding you
in its new arms.

The Photographer's Woman

"The search for truth is my obsession."
—Alfred Stieglitz

Describing the retrospective,
the curator said,
"She was always his woman.
But as you can see
in these newer photographs,
in the later years
she would not engage with him;
she looked off to the side,
was passive and resigned
because, familiar as they were
as man and wife, quite early on
he left her for another girl."

She saw no reason to look back;
in fact, the way she found to prove
she understood the need to set
precise focus, to calculate the angle
and measure the available light,
was to turn away from him,
to sit complacently while he
previewed depth of field
and fixed the aperture.

"In general, this is his exhibition,
clearly named, and through traveling
shows like this, he was the first
to claim photography as art.
But all the years she was the subject:
her face, her breast, her slender fingers
graced the plain gray space
of museum walls across the world."
They were her hands
that held the audience and gave
expression to sublime,
she was the muse through whose
vision he would chart
the pioneering map of his still art.
Yet, "he left her for another girl."

I have heard as he was dying
he called for her, and she came to him.
And I have thought, at last,
distant from public view,
in camera how they might have been
attracted once again to the roles
that those two played—
the encroaching shadow
and the ambient light—
in resolution and perspective,
in setting every final image right.

Poet to Painter

You ask me
how one can paint
the cries of seagulls.
In the same way,
I think I'd say, as one
can pen the colors
of morning or of night.

"How" is always full
of curiosity for me.
It's in the "why"
I find some certainty:
You paint, I write,
to move inside
the mysteries of light.

A Song of Ascent
for Hilary

That sultry afternoon I wandered off
to be alone and found some shade
beneath a short-arched colonnade
where fork-tailed, midnight-feathered birds
had set three muddy nests on the brick wall,
just where expert birders said I should expect,
since barn swallows prefer to nest
along hard surfaces man has made
and in neither the solitude of woods
nor in the soft shadowy places
where I choose to brood.

There in full view of me, and I of them,
they darted to a secret choreography—
deliberate swoops, majestic loops
the inverse of the neat architectural curves.
Bound to honor their instinctive trust,
beaks full of ration for the restless clutch,
they wheeled in earnest quiet, unable to sing.

That afternoon they broke all promises
with me, failed to give the one thing
the field guide, with authority, had assured:
a choric overture, an invitation sweet,
the familiar swallow's song,
liquid alarm call to *sleep, sleep, sleep* —
the one you know,
but was not meant for me.

As a Matter of Fact

the woman on the radio began
with cheerfulness and yet methodically
to explain the resonance
of nautilus and conch:
"more small cells," she said,
"more smooth-walled rooms
the richer tones
the shell transmutes
into the human ear
where small vibrations
slide through more delicate chambers
glide over natural curves
on the way to drum
where subtle outward hums
meet body sounds—
breath and pounding pulse.

"What's caught inside the shell
is not the voice of sea,"
she said with certainty,
"just so much clamor
made of cadences of other things:

"the singers on the radio
the cries of gulls
wind leaving lungs or rushing in
the hordes of shouting boys
run together into noise
that quakes in the air
breaks in the shell
makes waves of sound
against the ear
that only seem,"
she stressed again,
"like sound of waves."

"Not ocean at all"
were such simple words
to take the universe apart
snap imagination at the stem
and toss aside the marvels
that my mother handed down
beneath the rind of barnacles,
dismantle the only metaphor
my father ever found to hold
our present with the past
as they rolled out together
like future inexplicably
immense as sea.

Yet on she went
in her empiric way
swallowing the tails of words
her breath dissolving into pause
and changing tone to say
"we've reached conclusion for today
of the minute of discovery
wherein with science
we are unraveling
all the mysteries of our world."

And that was all
the time she had
she said with poise,
and yet I thought
with some regret,
to tease the truth
out of the noise.

"Remember it's not sea"
she voiced with pride
trailing off into the din
where knowledge tends to hide
the perfect melodies
that wonder sifts from tides
the siren songs it makes
as it echoes and falls and breaks
on the plain surfaces
of the only chambers she forgot
to look within—
the closest places
of the heart.

Mother of Moses

It was nothing that she said,
Nothing at all
That all these years
Has held me in her thrall.
It was in imagining
How valiantly she stood rocking him
Against destruction's tide,
Defying Pharaoh's hideous decree
And when she could no longer hide him
In her care with confidence
How she prepared the tiny ark
Out of papyrus and placed him there,
Knowing hope of deliverance
Would surely call Yahweh's children
To embark upon uncertain waters
Yet without impetuosity.

And so it was that she
In silence came to give him up
Into the river, into the hand
Of Him who is unspeakable
In mercy, power and name.
And so it was I saw
That for her part
She put aside captivity by faith
To wait the day.
Although she would not see
She knew the Hebrew women
Would all sing out
At once triumphantly
Of the twice parting of the reeds,
The way He led
The opening of sea.

Proper Words for Birds

Volery is a word I'm sure
my mother never used,
may have never heard,
although she always pointed out
the birds in flight, the places
they would light, knew every one
by name, found such riotous delight
in the way the cedar waxwings lay
on the winter ground between
Papa's house and ours, not dead
but drunk from stripping
the overripe fire orange berries
off the laden pyracantha branches
she espaliered along our brick wall.

Never did she tell us, if she knew,
that the several mourning doves
my father loved above the other birds
were strictly speaking a *piteousness*
whenever they came together;
nor would she ever have let on
that the masks distinguishing
the tiny ruby-crowned kinglets
and black-capped chickadees
might have been the very thing
that caused the ornithologists
to look upon their congregations
with so earnest a distrust as to term
them all together a *dissimulation*.

Mother's was a kind of understanding
that reached beyond the limits
of science and its strange taxonomy.
Mother always spoke to us
in other words about the birds:
"Listen," "Hush," "Come quickly
if you want to see the crazy nuthatch
creeping upside down again, there,
along the trunk of that maple tree."
"Watch," she would explain,
"when the hopping robin stops
and cocks her head toward the ground
it means she's found a tunneling worm
by the sound only the birds can hear."

So now when spring sends
migrating *parcel* after *parcel*
back from my native South,
reminiscence touches down in me
as a *descent* of flickers
to magnolia's glossy leaves.
Teakettle chants of Carolina wren
open memory and Mother's voice
floats back on each familiar note.
And I want to say in language
plain as I was taught,
"Mother, I have thought of you
when the redwings storm the marsh
and when the goldfinch sings."
I imagine she would answer me,
"I know you have and that you learned
without so many words
to apprehend the *charm*
of hummingbirds."

V

AND OF MEN

"A fool gives full vent to his spirit,
but a wise man quietly holds it back."

Proverbs 29:11

Unforeseen
for Chip

If the stag had not shot from his sentinel post
high on the beech-lined ridge and split
the cinder trail just one pace in front of you,
tossing his head in full careen so we would
see every point of his eight-tined rack before
he disappeared into the echoing ravine,
we would have passed through that October day
as heedless as every buck during the rut;
you would not have stopped short to ask if we
noticed how near and fast unforeseen danger
had dared to make such a casual pass before us;
and we would not have moved so attentively
into the hull of another man's timber;
I would never have heard your daughter say
"these look just like Papa's woods"
when we approached the place where
a wide creek meandered on past itself;
nor, after I forded first at the narrows
and looked back as you spread your feet
to keep everything in balance and reached
to guide her over the felled trunk,
would I have chanced to see in that flash,
as white-hot as the flame tail of the fleeing buck,
an afterimage of our father and me
and how closely the generations follow
when they encounter unfamiliar waters.

Paternal Instinct

My father was a man
who did not always have
a tool for every task
I brought to him,
yet when I asked
he always knew
how to fashion one
that we could use
from some other thing
that he found close
at hand.

What History Has to Say

The words are odd for Faulkner, I have always thought—
economic yet sufficient on their own, without the wandering
prose of *Absalom*, to describe the disengagement of students:
"with bovine interest." After these last days overlooking the
steep pasture lands and watching their movements, I question
his image at least with regard to the cattle. Because of how
they turn away from the sun, narrow their shadows in unison;
and then always come, as I approach, near the same corner of
the fence at the rim of the grassy plateau, as though to recover
year after year some familiar odor, truer than pheromone,
hidden deep within the layers of scent. This morning as they
moved to me, marvel settled in again and then the wondering—
if in their sensing they recalled the tilt of our heads, the lilt
of our voices as we spoke of them; if they remembered where
the shadows fell; if the sparrows crossed the path before us
that day; or if a sluicing wind made such a passing far too hard.
Or if that knot of them, kneeling in the cold pasture lined by old
cedars in the angling light, had seen what was between us then,
huddled behind clouds of breath too fine for the evening stillness
to distill. Now there seems nothing left, except to ask how you
became as Faulkner's students, though such point of view belies
your passion for the region's history. From your desk's vantage,
so distant now from scent and field, can you find a way to
contemplate what history has to say about whose recollections
can claim the past's closest hold?

Finding the Fisherman

My grandfather had hundreds of rose bushes,
an arm for casting,
a basement of rods, reeds, tackle,
a gray felt hat.
I was young
so I can't remember his stilled face,
glimpsed him only
moving through bed rows
teaching silence to blossom.

Saturdays his line cut the lake
luring bass to his earnest quiet.
Large and small-mouths,
bream and crappie
he won like roses,
brought them home clean
for our suppers,
left none for the taxidermist.

I keep his hat
and what likeness
I carry of him
through my father.
I look for more
in bushes burning to show me
in colors he grafted.
But winter is bloomless.

I find myself fisher casting for his image.
Always I hold too tightly
wait too late to release the line:
lure jerks in the wind
drops plumb to the ground.
I remember weekends
we were without him
and pull his felt brim down
to buffer the blast.

Lost in the Wilderness

What will you do
until the snow has melted
and the wilderness brightens
and opens herself to landing?

You cannot hide forever
in the wreckage of your body.
You cannot close your eyes
and lose your wetness,
your own dark wetness,
which presses shadows deep
into the frozen earth here
at the crossroads
of the empty wind.

The thick Alaskan hill
draws your body in
next to her cold thigh
where you could be content
to pour out all your secret life.

But stop, and in your waning
commit to memory the path
of drowsy snowflakes coming to rest,
the bluing lines on your sad hands,
the calculated flight
of circling willow ptarmigans
slowly coming brown,
the wolf and otter's tracks, the moon.
Commit all to yourself.

Lie down then in your aloneness
and memorize the earth
in all its ages and its coldness.
Lock yourself into the rock
of your freezing body into warmth.

Family Album

Each time she opens the tattered book
she finds herself drawn in
by the angle of her father's chin
and his before him
and how clearly even then
the dark-eyed boy gazed at the window
in a way that let her know
he longed to go, to leave
that set of jaw, that olive skin,
that name he shared with generations.
Each time, she studies once again
the subtle interplay of vision and of sight,
remembers how she pondered even then
what every turn of face might mean
and just what might become of him
when age had closed the shutter
and the only place to look
was in.

Note from the Good Land

Last Sunday as I waited to cross the one-lane bridge over
Tribulation Creek, which as you know this time of year is
never more than a filament of ice, tungsten-bright in the low
solstice light, threading the seam of the wadi, I wondered
again who named it. I would have asked you, but instead had
to imagine how you would have answered, pausing first, then
clearing your throat: "It must have been some squatter
making his way farther west than he had planned, because he
had seen a small band of Monacans at a distance. A young
man, no doubt, who knew little of history and even less about
Powhatan's help; who was already weary from his lone ardor
in hunting the right place to settle; who'd come by then to
understand that, even in this good and broad land, so much
runs to the contrary—the ancient New River and its odd
tributaries flow westward for no other reason than to defy
the rule of the Continental Divide, and trails that seem worn
through the tangle of underbrush clear down to the bare
ground come to nothing more than random conclusions.

By that point I had made the first hairpin back toward the east
where the vista opens. There they were again, that elusive
flock of crows, this time fluttering against the tenebrous sky
like a satin cloak as luminously black as the ravens of Cherith,
descending on the cornfields, knowing just where to glean, no
longer strange sojourners in our wasteland of broken stalks.

Meredith's Law

> *It is this way with verse and animals*
> *And love, that when you point you lose them all.*
> —William Meredith, "Sonnet on Rare Animals"

You say you have never understood
poetry so there's no hope in searching
out a cure for your confusion.
I should just let it lie.
I think I can convince you otherwise
when I show you how it seems
Meredith shared our passion
for the animals. William Meredith,
I mean. He said it in his poetry:
It is this way with verse and animals
And love, that when you point you lose them all.
Surely you consent to that from experience—
how when we stroll the old boardwalk
beside the swamp, the river otter always slips
beneath the current's curl and hummingbird
flees the full hibiscus cup at our approach.
We can always be certain of that much
loss before we ever begin. *It is this way. . .*
That much is true, you say.
Before you turn away let me continue
to suggest that if you take a moment
to palpate his lines, you just may uncover
something as remarkable beneath the skin
of words as your trained hands sometimes
find when you press viscera.

That said, I am willing to admit
that *verse and animals* may seem to be
an extremely awkward coupling at first.
But if you let that notion lie awhile,
I think you'll see how a poet's speech
can make some sense out of things
when plainer words cannot.
And love . . . love is another thing—
a hackneyed word, often absurd
in the ways we use it
and always in its cost;
but I trust you will agree
it is as unfathomable as *verse*
and maybe even will admit
that those two could be twins,
even when you think just one
of them is worthy of pursuit.
I see at last I've moved you
to my side and am ecstatic
when you finally say,
if you are understanding Meredith,
it's senseless for us to go on this way.
I think you mean *Our meddling*
intellect misshapes the beauteous
forms of things—we murder to dissect.
I agree, most certainly we do,
although I dare not tell you now
that Wordsworth thought so too.

Mending

By practicing alone
the steadfast angler learns
not only where to set each line
to lure the fish, but as sure
as the old trout—
torn-finned, stream-wary,
caught and released again—
to sense the course
of warmest rill;
to fathom every quiet depth
of patient skill it takes
to master an expectant cast;
to lay aside the need
to ask again why he
must mend so constantly
against the current flow.

A Neighbor in the Aftermath

For years I watched my neighbor
groom his piece of land
and never say a word and yet
I marveled at the way his hands
would gently pat the dirt around the bulb,
how neat and round he clipped the shrubs,
how straight he pushed the mower across the grass.

He never stopped to talk nor I to ask
what he thought of anything
except a few days in the aftermath
of the bright September blight that left us dumb.
And he too stood at first silent and still
leaning on the handle of his hoe,
then pulled off his hat and gloves
as if to show respect
before he pointed to the bed
and with more eloquence
than I imagined he possessed,
he simply said:

"Look at the way
I have always arranged the plants
just as my father did—
the smaller ones against the edge,
the taller ones in back, and all of them
laid out in patterns by their hue.
And surely passersby do stop amazed
at what they say's the constant beauty of my place,
which, by the way, leads to one observation
today I feel obliged to make:
What we have always called perennial
of course is not and never was.
Each gardener knows every blossom
drops one way or another
victim to its fleeting season
or to sleet or drought,
and what opens next
year on the slender shoots,
although quite similar,
are different blooms
drenched in another light.

"But I digress; it was this I had to say:
Sometimes when I work my yard
I look beyond, out where I see
the hundred textures, thousand tints of green—
and there's a wonder in the way
the rough winds seed the field
in broad array like love and grief,
the way the leaves are not raked clean,
the way the flowers are not in bordered beds
or ordered color schemes,
the way it makes vast perfect gardens
that need neither trowel nor hands."
And then like that he stopped,
pulled on his gloves
and slipped back into his hat.

This year his winter garden
is much finer than the last—
Burford hollies thick with berries,
rows of pansies manicured,
some blossoms fully open,
other buds still holding tight.
When I pass his house
I simply try to match my gaze
with his, the way that it goes out
past the corner of the neat stone edge.

Last Dance

Stand here with me at the mountain
meadow's high edge and watch:
now that the longest days have gone
once more and the monarchs,
which through spring and summer
came to lay or feed on them,
have flown away to winter
in more temperate zones,
these milkweed stalks no longer bend
one by one to the mere dependency
of those fluttering throngs.
Instead they lean in unison
as though bowing in homage
to a beckoning wind, succumb
to the tendril tongue of autumn sun
that coaxes them to open spindle pods
wide enough to free from husky hold
the myriad white-feathered seeds
that they expel like a last breath
across the rustling fields; and those,
their promise and their progeny,
waltz the saffron day away
taken up on highland melodies.
Although we cannot hear them now,
my love, I want us to imagine
how our final dance might be
as light as theirs, how we will float
above the stony ground, following
another secret music, bound to find
its origin hidden within a single note.

VI

THE WISDOM OF CREATURES

"But ask the beasts and they will teach you,
or the birds of the heavens, and they will tell you."

Job 12:7

Drake

Even as spring
snails across the pond
I see the mallard stand
in the deepening hollow
without a hen.
And I imagine
when summer dries the meadow
he alone will go
to search another place
to satisfy his twilight longings.

But night and then dawn
passing again and again
I see that lone drake
standing still in the hollow.
And I trust this time
when the clouds clear
he will take wing
sensing finally what light to follow
to navigate the passage
of a narrow season,
explore remoter realms
of solitude.

Fallow Field

The cows have lost interest
in the mountain range
fail to see the resemblance
of slopes' bowed silhouettes
to their own bone backs
and turn instead
to watch a sallow light
descend behind
a shrinking pond
where the dusky bull
stands to his neck
in brown water.
Following him in
they send slow currents
to stroke his heavy flanks.
Roused, he looks up
finds his own image
in the black foothills
beyond them
and wades back
drops to his knees
in a fallow field
dreaming himself sire
before the darkness.

Unseen

Throughout the morning
the ordinary ravens
craving notice circle
and hurl their shadows
on hard March ground.
In the broad afternoon
some invisible bird,
trilling an unfamiliar tune,
hides in the privet, forsythia,
curly willow, oak, poplar, pine,
incites our curiosity,
invites us to come outside
to find it, frame it, call it
by its common name,
claim to know its song.
After hours of searching,
watching, waiting,
traipsing the close woods,
none of us can,
no one at all.

Pastoral

Late day again in the ochre field:
black and white calf is open-faced
beside the one rolled bale
where his cow always finds satiety
in the spare hold of golden straw.
Neither takes any note of me
watching from the frozen edge
of this bare pastoral tableau.
He stares while she ruminates.
Neither takes note of anything
until a vagrant slate-colored cat
hard from winter and wood bound
moves through their sloping pasture
without sound and crosses down
beyond her line of vision
to the blind of brush and yellow pine.
Under the roll of pallid clouds
that pull the tattered tarp of dusk,
bland winter's blank wide awning,
he takes her udder and he sups.
Late day, they seem simply content
to stand vacant in this place
and wait one more sure dawning.

An Offering

Out of this abundance
of birds
only the tiny one,
the skittish
and skittering
Carolina wren,
the one of constant
flittering, black, white,
small as widow's mite,
dares come
to my window
to feed, grows still,
bows to the sill,
picks the smallest
yellow seed
but leaves the greater
offering, a harbinger
of bright paschal hope
come down
on slightest wing.

Snail's Pace

If there had been any options then, perhaps
that first snail's own selection would have
been naturally to choose its deliberate
pace, even to conspire to slow its race
to make its glide seem smooth and
to hide what it must have sensed
right from the start how both
in its leisure and in its labor
it is one inexorable slide
through which inch by
every inch another
small part of
itself melts
slowly
away.

White Noise

They say in truth
a white bear's fur
is not white by itself
but steals its color
scattering reflected light,
the same as snow, as ice.
Pristine magnificence of polar bear
reclining cumbrous on the caps,
fishing deftly from the floes,
lies in fur's transparent cores.
Then eye's echo,
persistent white noise,
creates what seems pure form.
The substance of it is
accepting emptiness
as being filled.

Lowing

The first night
twilight like a tender bruise
purpled on the screen and deepened
until it took the silhouettes
of fence posts and the farm.

In the morning
men slipped in past the wires
with cotton neck ropes
to ring the heifer
and lead it from its mother's side
to the bed of their truck
softened with hay
and to the valley beyond.

We asked one man.
He said the bands
around the woolly worms
weren't wide and full;
the winter would be mild.
He said the cow
might cry a month
until she forgot.

Frost was early that year
and the blankets
and windows came down.
Yet through it all
we could hear the cow.

Witness

Beside the pasture this morning
I witnessed the anticipation
of the one waiting horse turn
to what seemed disappointment
at the discovery of my empty hand
while the second small stallion watched
content from behind the frosty nimbus
of his breath before they thundered off
together, whinnying, to find satiety
in new grass and withered shoot,
not harnessed by the question
around which we so aimlessly trot
of how to make every desire
our own private possession.
For them in their land of plenty
sufficiency is always a given,
for what is given is sufficient.

VII

WHAT ABIDES

"So now faith, hope, love abide; these three."
1 Corinthians 13:13

Certain Light

So dark may come for me,
The compelling evidence suggests,
As relentlessly as dusk
When ambient light subsides,
And time peels field of vision back
And tunnel tapers into black
And eye resigns itself
Beneath the heft of my inheritance.

I have seen twilight fall each day,
A fleeting harbinger of night,
Itself impermanent, which bows
Before sure planetary lights
That find the narrow breach
In dark's broad wall
And then array their luminance
Against the midnight pall.

Before depravity of shadow enters in,
Commences its hard press on me
And all the frailties of my sight,
I am resolved to look beyond myself
As moons for eons have
To find the source of constant light
By which is marked their course
Of praise, the glory they reflect.

So shall I defy this curse of blindness
Poised to destroy my fragile eye
Which, looking in, is weak and focus dim
But looking out and fixed on Him
Makes vision strong and magnifies the hope
And faith through which redeems
The promise that He made to me:
All the certain light that I shall need.

Come Now

Come now
and do not hesitate
the hour is late
and time we should go in:
make the night watch
open the shade
take off our shoes
and wait the morning.

Come closer now
so you can see:
she has joyfully thrown off
the white coat of her sorrow
could not wait until tomorrow
to chase the light
dance barefoot, agile, bright
across the dew-dressed fields.

Come away now
and let us attend
to what we must
find the way to trust
what winnowed hearts discern:
it is a sacred grace
to slip into the place
for which she wholly yearned.

Keeping Silence

The mist distills
in strands of luminous beads
along the quivering lips of leaves
poised to tell their vain imaginings,
secrets hidden sole within their keep:
what sends the sleek red foxes
back into their lairs
before the day descends;
or what it is that moves
beyond the trees
when what it is that moves
is more than breeze;
why moonlight never
has the strength
to make the stars recede.
Old oaks are poised to give
their own account of these.
Yet silence is their inheritance,
a sacred bond they cannot break
until wind wills to turn
leaves into holy instruments,
instill the gift as tongues
by which they whisper, trill,
sing its songs, then tremble
into quiet once again
before they heed its one last call
to fall burnished, without toil,
transform the barrenness
of autumn's muted soil.

Contemplating Pluto

From where we stand the cobalt skies
seem the same as they were last night
and all the major constellations
as children we could name remain
in view and shimmer as they have
throughout our lives and one day's
movement of shadow across the moon
is imperceptible to our naked eyes.
But international astronomers by consensus
have declared it time to revise the universe,
to redefine what *planet* in our solar system
means, and although the celestial bodies
all run their same expected orbits of the sun,
the designation will be stripped from one.
Thus history repeats itself again
as Pluto's demotion renders youthful
memory, as well as Holtz's suite of seven
planets, whole once more, complete,
and warring Mars, out of order,
still assumes the lead.

Gradual Song

I think it would be better
If the death of things,
Of almost everything—
Of tree and dream and memory
Of friendship and of love—
Were furious and sudden
And not gradual as fall.

Suffrages

(sotto voce)

In the iridescent dust of monarch's wing
and secret places of my brokenness
In the turquoise ring encircling gannet's eye
and secret places of my brokenness
In the frost's filigrees that edge the alder leaves
and secret places of my brokenness
In slim filament of spider's fragile weave
and secret places of my brokenness
In the glide of snail along the lilting stalk
and secret places of my brokenness
In spotted ensatina's slide between the rocks
and secret places of my brokenness
In cypress shadow's fall in darkening bog
and secret places of my brokenness
In slow peep of dawn that breaches vernal fog
and secret places of my brokenness
In minuscule grain of sand that seeds the pearl
and secret places of my brokenness
In deep yellow bruise that stains the wind-bent reed
and secret places of my brokenness
In all of these things, in all of them, in all
when I lie quiet I hear your still voice call.

What the Mountain Knows

Three things are too wonderful for me;
four I do not understand.
—Proverbs 30:18

Mountain, there are three things you know
that I have long held in wonder;
the fourth, perhaps together we can ponder.

First, did primal light have a regular pace as it broke
across your face and was there music when
moon and stars aligned above your brow each night?

Second, was it the wind that taught the wolf
to howl or did the wolf give voice to the wind
and could you hear it then—the wind,

I mean—before the low-meadowed places
were filled with the reeds and nimble grasses
it could trill beneath its long green breath?

Third, as you watched leaves twist and flutter
and clouds race and rushing currents refuse
to break over the small stones they smoothed,

did you ever long for what seemed like the power
of wind and water as they made their fleeting prowess
known by moving things and then by moving on?

Fourth, when pulse of light at last grows far
too faint to paint the valley floor and weary wind
wanders off beside the sullen wolf and water leaves

---

its riverbeds unmade and saplings and old trees
relinquish every leaf and lake turns into glade,
where will you look to find your still reflection?

Epitaph

I hope my life was penned
in such a way that when time
comes to write my epitaph
someone might think to say
not that I was good so much
as kind and that I wrote
quite well beyond my means
because it was the wind of grace
blown down that gave me words
and moved my sluggish hands,
and that I always sought
to know the unseen things,
and though I loved the breadth
of language for my art,
my heart always seemed fixed
on a day when all the sound
and words would fall away,
and that I was quite hopeful
to the last if anyone would choose
one line to inscribe my memory
in stone it surely should be
the simple supposition I know right:
there merely is no synonym for light.

Divinum Mysterium

It is all about light:
the way it rises and it rests
the way it can distinguish
a forest from its trees
and dissect the delicate spaces
between the limbs and leaves
and put soft shadows down
along the woodland floor.

It is all about light:
the way it seeks a silhouette
the way it can transform
the rough and round
to smooth and plain
and create a clean horizon
with the indelible stain
that makes perspective black and white.

It is all about light:
the way it carries itself
the way the distant stellar beams
regardless of how slight
refuse to take their cover
in the heavy shroud of night
the way even the smallest flame
can push the darkness out.

In the beginning
and in the end
it is all about light.

Paraclete Poetry Series Editor
Mark S. Burrows

ACKNOWLEDGMENTS

Grateful acknowledgement is given to the editors of the following literary journals in which many of the poems in this volume, some in slightly different forms, previously appeared: *Alaska Quarterly Review, Appalachian Heritage, Avocet, The Baltimore Review, Borderlands, Buckle &, California Quarterly Review, The Cape Rock Review, Chicago Quarterly Review, Chrysalis Reader, Confluence, Crucible, Diner, ep;phany, The Evansville Review, Flyway: A Literary Review, Frigg Magazine, The Griffin, GW Review, Hampden-Sydney Poetry Review, The Hurricane Review, Limestone, Louisiana Literature, Lumina, Manzanita, Minnetonka Review, Mother Earth International Journal, New Delta Review, Nimrod International Journal, North Atlantic Review, Pembroke Magazine, Phoebe, Plainsongs, Poem, Poet Lore, River Oak Review, RiverSedge, Schuylkill Valley Journal, SLANT: A Journal of Poetry, Slow Trains, Softblow, Soundings East, South Carolina Review, Talking River Review, Tiger's Eye: A Journal of Poetry, Westview, Wisconsin Review,* and *Whiskey Island Magazine.*

Thanks are also offered to Ted Kooser, editor of *The Windflower Home Almanac of Poetry* in which "Lowing" first appeared, and to the publisher and editors of Finishing Line Press, publisher of my chapbook *Proper Words for Birds* in which sixteen of these poems first appeared.

Special gratitude belongs to the Virginia Center for Creative Arts (VCCA) that has provided me numerous residential Fellowships over the years. Many of the poems in this volume would not have come into being without the gift of uninterrupted time in that creative space.

Finally, whole-hearted gratitude is offered to Virginia artist Gray S. Dodson, who graciously offered her magnificent painting Light Play II as the cover art for this book.

ABOUT THE AUTHOR

Poet and photographer Margaret B. Ingraham was born in Atlanta, Georgia, and "grew up" exploring the woods behind her childhood home. She is the author of a poetry chapbook *Proper Words for Birds* (Finishing Line Press), nominated for the 2010 Library of Virginia Award in poetry, and of *This Holy Alphabet* (Paraclete Press), lyric poems adapted from her original translation from the Hebrew of Psalm 119. Ingraham is the recipient of an Academy of American Poetry Award, a Sam Ragan Prize, and numerous residential Fellowships at the Virginia Center for the Creative Arts. She has been a guest lecturer on poetry and the psalms at Wesley Theological Seminary in Washington, DC, and the Virginia Theological Seminary, and has twice collaborated with internationally recognized composer Gary Davison, most notably to create "Shadow Tides," a choral symphony commissioned by Artistic Director Gretchen Kuhrmann for *Choralis* to commemorate the tenth anniversary of 9/11 and performed on that date in 2011 in Washington, DC. Ingraham resides in Alexandria, Virginia.

ABOUT PARACLETE PRESS

WHO WE ARE

As the publishing arm of the Community of Jesus, Paraclete Press presents a full expression of Christian belief and practice—from Catholic to Evangelical, from Protestant to Orthodox, reflecting the ecumenical charism of the Community and its dedication to sacred music, the fine arts, and the written word. We publish books, recordings, sheet music, and video/DVDs that nourish the vibrant life of the church and its people.

WHAT WE ARE DOING

BOOKS

PARACLETE PRESS BOOKS show the richness and depth of what it means to be Christian. While Benedictine spirituality is at the heart of who we are and all that we do, our books reflect the Christian experience across many cultures, time periods, and houses of worship.

We have many series, including *Paraclete Essentials*; *Paraclete Fiction*; *Paraclete Poetry*; *Paraclete Giants*; and for children and adults, *All God's Creatures*, books about animals and faith; and *San Damiano Books*, focusing on Franciscan spirituality. Others include *Voices from the Monastery* (men and women monastics writing about living a spiritual life today), *Active Prayer*, and new for young readers: *The Pope's Cat*. We also specialize in gift books for children on the occasions of Baptism and First Communion, as well as other important times in a child's life, and books that bring creativity and liveliness to any adult spiritual life.

The MOUNT TABOR BOOKS series focuses on the arts and literature as well as liturgical worship and spirituality; it was created in conjunction with the Mount Tabor Ecumenical Centre for Art and Spirituality in Barga, Italy.

MUSIC

The PARACLETE RECORDINGS label represents the internationally acclaimed choir *Gloriæ Dei Cantores*, the *Gloriæ Dei Cantores Schola*, and the other instrumental artists of the *Arts Empowering Life Foundation*.

Paraclete Press is the exclusive North American distributor for the Gregorian chant recordings from St. Peter's Abbey in Solesmes, France. Paraclete also carries all of the Solesmes chant publications for Mass and the Divine Office, as well as their academic research publications.

In addition, PARACLETE PRESS SHEET MUSIC publishes the work of today's finest composers of sacred choral music, annually reviewing over 1,000 works and releasing between 40 and 60 works for both choir and organ.

VIDEO

Our video/DVDs offer spiritual help, healing, and biblical guidance for a broad range of life issues including grief and loss, marriage, forgiveness, facing death, understanding suicide, bullying, addictions, Alzheimer's, and Christian formation.

Learn more about us at our website:
www.paracletepress.com
or phone us toll-free at 1.800.451.5006

SCAN
TO
READ
MORE

Hungry Spring and Ordinary Song:
Collected Poems

Phyllis Tickle

ISBN 978-1-61261-788-6 | $18

Eye of the Beholder

Luci Shaw

ISBN 978-1-64060-085-0 | $18

POEMS

THE
CONSEQUENCE
OF MOONLIGHT

SOFIA STARNES

The Consequence of Moonlight

Sofia Starnes

ISBN 978-1-61261-860-9 | $18

Available at bookstores
Paraclete Press 1-800-451-5006
www.paracletepress.com